Other Book
by
Veletta A. Butcher

Nonfiction
50 Year Old Love Letters (A Two-fold Love Story)

Crumbs
from the
Master's
Table

Veletta Butcher

ISBN: 978-1-6847-1557-2 (sc)
ISBN: 978-1-6847-1558-9 (e)

All Scripture quotations are taken from THE MESSAGE, copyright © 1993, 2002, 2018 by Eugene H. Peterson. Used by permission of NavPress. All rights reserved. Represented by Tyndale House Publishers, a Division of Tyndale House Ministries.

Lulu Publishing Services rev. date: 01/17/2020

Dedicated to

My parents, Fred D. and Lalage (Prewett) Fussell

And

My Father-in-law W.H. (Henry) Butcher and
Mother-in-law Fannie Butcher

For without these four people in my life, I
would not be where I am today.

These dear loved ones are the reason I have a spiritual legacy.

Contents

Acknowledgements

Want to thank two of my four siblings
For support once again in helping me
Accomplish the completion of another book.
First my sister, Catherine Fussell-Dreiss, for making sure I said it right.
And my brother, Jeffery Fussell, for getting me
through all the technology maze once again.

Preface

"And she said, Truth, Lord: yet the dogs eat of the crumbs which fall from their masters' table." Matthew 15:27

Crumbs? Have you ever considered that a crumb contains all the ingredients used in the batter of the whole loaf or baked goods? I heard Rev. C.M. Becton make this statement in a sermon he preached using the example of the Syrophenician woman.

In the last few years, during my devotions, God has dropped into my heart thoughts that I have called "crumbs." These reminded me of the scripture of the Syrophenician woman and her response to Jesus, "Truth, Lord: yet the dogs eat of the crumbs which fall from their masters' table." (Matthew 15:27.) In her hour of need and brokenness she came to the Savior. Likewise, in my hour of need, the Lord began to bless me with "crumbs" that fell from His bountiful table.

As you read each one, the Lord may drop thoughts into your heart, so a page is provided after each one for you to write your thoughts.

May you enjoy and be blessed and encouraged.

Veletta A. Butcher
December 2019

A Safe Place

A Safe Place

"The Lord is our rock and a refuge; a safe place in the time of trouble" (II Samuel 22:1-3).

When we were children, home was a safe place after dark. At dusk, Mother would call for us to come in from play, and we felt secure within the bounders of the principles and disciplines our mothers instilled in us. But, our only real safe place is in the arms of the Savior. God is our refuge and protection during the storms and trials of life.

Even now, in my later years, I have felt insecure at times. It is a scary place when you wonder how to handle situations beyond your strength, capabilities or finances. Then is when you can run to that safe place in the Lord. But how do we 'run' into that safe place with God? Or how can He teach us to depend on Him? It is when we go to God in prayer and ask for direction and guidance in times of trouble and when we open the Bible and read his word, "casting all your care on him; for He careth for you." (I Peter 5:7.)

What comfort to read scriptures and find that "The name of the Lord is a strong tower: the righteous runneth into it, and is safe." (Proverbs 18:10.) Or that "The eternal God is thy refuge, and underneath are the everlasting arms…" (Deut. 33:27). Or, "…when my heart is overwhelmed: lead me to the Rock that is higher than I. Thou hast been a shelter for me, and a strong tower from the enemy." (Psalm 61:2-3.)

We also read the words of Jesus, "Come unto me all ye that labor and are heavy laden, and I will give you rest. Take my yoke upon you, and learn of me; for I am meek and lowly in heart: and ye shall find rest unto your souls. For my yoke is easy, and my burden is light." (Matthew 11:28-30.)

What assurance that we can always find a safe place within the tower of refuge, Jesus Christ, our Savior. Therefore, when life overwhelms us, let us run to the Rock that is on high, a safe place in the times of trouble.

For Your Own Personal Thoughts

A Pillar in the House of the Lord

A Pillar in the House of the Lord

Pillar or Pilaster is a firm upright, support, for a superstructure consisting of a base, shaft, and capital. The base is the support or foundation of the bottom of the column or shaft part of the pillar. The capital crowns the shaft and takes on the weight of the entablature, or upper section of a wall or story. (Definition from Webster's Dictionary)

A minister once asked all those in the congregation to stand if they had been in the church fifty years or more. He then said, "These are the pillars of the church."

To compare the spiritual life of an individual to a pillar would mean they are the primary support in the house of God. First, they would have to have a foundation (base) in Jesus Christ. The shaft or column might represent their life and lifestyle patterned after godly and righteous living. The capital, which takes the weight of the upper structure, could serve to represent the spiritual atmosphere they bring into the house of God, giving support to the ministry and the preaching of the gospel.

Galatians 2:9, "And when James, Cephas, and John, who seemed to be pillars, perceived the grace that was given unto me, they gave to me and Barnabas the right hands of fellowship..."

In I Timothy 3:15, Paul admonished Timothy to behave himself in the house of God as a pillar grounded in truth.

And in Revelation, we note that God will make those who overcome, pillars in His temple.

"Him that overcometh will I make a pillar in the temple of my God ...." (Revelation 3:12).

What an honor for one to become a pillar in the house of the Lord.

For Your Own Personal Thoughts

A Sure Foundation

A Sure Foundation

Jesus said in John 5:39, "Search the scriptures; for in them ye think you have eternal life: and they are they that testify of me." At the time Jesus spoke this, they only had the Old Testament; today, we have the New Testament as well as the Old. Let us make sure of our foundation whereon we build.

I Timothy 6:17-19, "Charge them that are rich in this world, that they be not high-minded, nor trust in uncertain riches, but in the living God, who giveth us richly all things to enjoy; … laying up in store for themselves a good foundation against the time to come, that they may lay hold on eternal life."

Proverbs 23:23, "Buy the truth and sell it not; also wisdom, and instruction, and understanding."

I Corinthians 3: 11-15
"For other foundation can no man lay than that is laid, which is Jesus Christ. (v.11)
Any man build upon this foundation (Jesus Christ).
Gold, silver, precious stones (spiritual/heavenly/eternal)
Wood, hay, stubble (carnal/earthly/temporal)
Every man's work will be made manifest
The day shall declare it
Because will be revealed by fire
The fire will try every man's work of what sort it is (eternal/temporal).

If any man's work abide that he has built upon (the
foundation – Jesus Christ)
He will receive a reward.
If any man's work is burned,
He will suffer loss
But he himself shall be saved
Yet so as by fire.

I realized when reading this scripture; there is no "or," or "and"
between the words gold, silver, precious stones, wood, hay, stubble. We
all will have some of each since we live in a fallen world. At times I have
built with wood, hay, stubble on my foundation, Jesus Christ. However,
at other times I have laid some gold, silver, precious stones on it. Will I
have more of the gold, silver, precious stones, or will I have entangled my
life in earthly things?

Let us then build upon Jesus Christ, the chief cornerstone of the
foundation. "Repent and be baptized every one of you in the name of
Jesus Christ for the remission of sins, and ye shall receive the gift of the
Holy Ghost." (Acts 2:38.)

For Your Own Personal Thoughts

_____

_____

_____

_____

_____

_____

_____

_____

_____

_____

_____

_____

_____

Beauty of the Church

Beauty of the Church

In Exodus chapters 26 and 27, we find God told Moses to build the Tabernacle and cover the outside with badger skins. I am sure that did not look too appealing to the human eye. But the instructions He gave for the inside was very ornate and beautiful: carved work, tapestries of fine linen, of blue, scarlet and purple, needlework and things of gold and brass. These are all pleasant to the eye.

From without, there is no beauty to the church. When the carnal man looks at the church of the living God, he is not impressed. He still has a hard time seeing the glory of the church.

But when the spiritual man sees the church, he sees the glorious blessings bestowed upon man. He is aware of wonderful peace and contentment, the promises of eternal life, the Shekinah glory, the Holy Ghost, and the hope of heaven.

Through spiritual eyes, it's more like a view of Solomon's magnificent Temple: ivory and beaten work, carved pomegranates and palm trees, and all kinds of things of gold, hangings of scarlet, blue and purple and fine twined linen. The Queen of Sheba was even taken back at the grandeur and magnificence of it.

Are you looking at the rough badger skins, and rams' skins dyed red, or the beautiful needlework of blue, purple, scarlet and fine linen, light of candlestick; anointing oil; sweet incense; smell of the spices of anointing oil; gold, silver, vessels of brass; priests garments; mercy-seat; cherubim, the ark, the table of showbread, altar of burnt offering, laver of brass, and jewels in the breastplate and the ephod? (Found in Exodus 35: 11-19, 26-28, 30-35; Exodus 36: 8, 19-20, 35, 37.)

Our vessels of flesh, when God fills us with His presence; this is the beauty of the church.

"What? Know ye not that your body is the temple of the Holy Ghost which is in you, which ye have of God, and ye are not your own? For ye are bought with a price: therefore glorify God in your body, and in your spirit, which are God's." (I Corinthians 6:19-20.)

For Your Own Personal Thoughts

Be of Good Cheer

Be of Good Cheer

There are only seven references in the Bible that say, "Be of good cheer." Five, our Lord Jesus Christ spoke. Each time these words were spoken, the situation at the moment was uncertain, frightening, turbulent, or despairing.

Matthew and Mark both recorded the story of the disciples out in the midst of the sea in a great storm when Jesus came walking on water, and they were afraid of what they saw as well as the storm that raged around them.

"But straightway Jesus spake unto them, saying, Be of good cheer; it is I; be not afraid." (Matthew 14:27.) "For they all saw him, and were troubled. And immediately he talked with them, and saith unto them, Be of good cheer: it is I; be not afraid." (Mark 6:50.)

John told the story of what we call the last supper. Jesus and his disciples had just left the last meal he would have with them before his betrayal, mock trial, crucifixion, and burial. Not a time that they would think as being cheerful.

"These things I have spoken unto you, that in me ye might have peace. In the world ye shall have tribulation: but be of good cheer; I have overcome the world." (John 16:33.)

Matthew told of four friends who brought to Jesus, a man, lying on a bed, sick of the palsy. Even in our disability and despair, Jesus speaks peace. "And, behold, they brought to him a man sick of the palsy, lying on a bed: and Jesus seeing their faith said unto the sick of the palsy; Son, be of good cheer; thy sins be forgiven thee." (Matthew 9:2.) In the gospel of Mark 2: 1-12, this same story is told in more detail.

In Acts, we read that Paul was in the midst of a storm on his way to Rome, and the Lord spoke to him. God was with him and would bring Paul safely through the storm. And Paul also admonished those in the ship to be of good cheer.

"And the night following the Lord stood by him, and said, Be of good cheer, Paul: for as thou hast testified of me in Jerusalem, so must thou bear witness also at Rome." (Acts 23:11.)

"And now I (Paul) exhort you to be of good cheer: for there shall be no loss of any man's life among you, but of the ship. For there stood by me this night the angel of God, whose I am, and whom I serve, saying, Fear not, Paul; thou must be brought before Caesar: and, lo, God hath given thee all them that sail with thee. Wherefore, sirs, be of good cheer: for I believe God, that it shall be even as it was told me." (Acts 27:22-25.)

Jesus never promised us there would not be any storms in our lives, but He did promise to be with us.

We can take heart and "Be of good cheer," because we have read the back of the Book and we win if we stay close to the Lord.

For Your Own Personal Thoughts

_____

_____

_____

_____

_____

_____

_____

_____

_____

_____

_____

_____

_____

_____

Beware of Worldview

Beware of Worldview

Paul's warning in Colossians 2:8 can be applied to us today to beware of the worldview.

Be warned because:

"As ye have therefore received Christ Jesus the Lord, so walk ye in him: rooted and built up in him, and stablished in the faith, as ye have been taught, abounding therein with thanksgiving." (Colossians 2:6-7.)

Therefore, we are told to, "Beware lest any man spoil you

Through philosophy (*Practical or moral wisdom, ethics*)

Vain (*empty, devoid of real value; useless; worthless*)

Deceit (*mislead; tricky; fraudulent; delude*),

After traditions (*beliefs and customs handed down from the past*) of men,

After rudiments (*that which is underdeveloped*) of the world,

And not after Christ." (Colossians 2:8.)

Jesus even warned his disciples to be not deceived: By false witnesses: "For out of the heart proceed ..., false witness, blasphemies:" (Matthew 15:19.); by false Christs and false prophets:

"For false Christs and false prophets shall rise...." (Mark 13:22.)

The apostle Peter also warned to be not deceived: By false teachers: "... Even as there shall be false teachers among you...." (II Peter 2:1-2.)

And Paul again warned to be not deceived: By false apostles: "For such are false apostles... And no marvel; for Satan himself is transformed into an angel of light." (II Corinthians 11:13-14.) ; By false Brethren: "And that because of false brethren unawares brought in...." (Galatians 2:4.)

But by the Spirit of truth, we have eternal life. For Jesus prayed, "Sanctify them through thy truth: thy word is truth." (John 17:17.)

Therefore, having obeyed Acts 2:38 (repented, baptized in Jesus name, and filled with the Holy Ghost), we hold fast to the faith.

And Jude wrote, "Beloved, when I gave all diligence to write unto you of the common salvation, it was needful for me to write unto you, and exhort you that ye should earnestly contend for the faith which was once delivered unto the saints.…..But ye, beloved, building up yourselves on your most holy faith, praying in the Holy Ghost, keep yourselves in the love of God, looking for the mercy of our Lord Jesus Christ unto eternal life." (Jude 1:3, 20-21.)

"For in him (*Jesus Christ*) dwelleth all the fullness of the Godhead bodily." (Colossians 2:9.)

For Your Own Personal Thoughts

Crown Jewels

Crown Jewels

Have you ever thought about the world's "crown jewels" secured behind heavy glass and tight security where authorities guard them from theft?

In the book of Malachi, the Lord refers to those who belong to him as jewels.

Malachi's message came after they had restored the Temple, and yet the people and priests did not reverence the Lord of hosts. Therefore, God was challenging them to trust him, and he would pour out blessings beyond their wildest dreams

And in this setting, we find the following verses:

"Then they that feared the LORD spake often one to another:
and the LORD hearkened, and heard it,
and a book of remembrance was written before him for them that feared the LORD,
and that thought upon his name.
And they shall be mine, saith the LORD of hosts, in that day when I make up my jewels, and I will spare them, as a man spareth his own son that serveth him." (Malachi 3:16-17.)

God has secured his own "crown jewels" with His very blood. Protecting with his blood against the thief who goes about as a roaring lion, seeking whom he may devour. (See I Peter 5:8.)

God has written a book of remembrance with the names of those who fear him and think upon his name declaring they are his "crown jewels."

The world's "crown jewels" cannot compare with God's "jewels" who have, and do, walk among us daily.

For Your Own Personal Thoughts

_____

_____

_____

_____

_____

_____

_____

_____

_____

_____

_____

_____

_____

_____

_____

Decision for the Better

Decision for the Better

We make many decisions every day. Most of them seem unimportant. However, some have the power to change the course of our lives forever.

Recorded in the Bible are some individuals who made decisions by faith that changed their destinies and influenced future generations.

There was Abraham for one. He decided to leave Ur of the Chaldees and follow God. "By faith Abraham, when he was called to go out into a place which he should after receive for an inheritance, obeyed…." (Hebrews 11:8). Because of that decision, there is the nation of Israel today. What magnitude that one decision Abraham made so long ago.

If today we could interview Abraham, what would be his reply? One thing I am sure would be how grateful he is that God chose him out of all peoples and that eternity will not be long enough to praise and thank God for all His lovingkindness and blessings.

Another individual was Ruth, the Moabite, who chose to follow her mother-in-law, Naomi, back to Bethlehem. "And Ruth said, entreat me not to leave thee, or to return from following after thee…" (Ruth 1:16). Because of her decision, she is listed in the lineage of King David, and ultimately of Jesus Christ. (see Matthew 1:5.) At the time, she had no idea the significance that decision would have on generations to come.

And today, if we could interview Ruth what would be her reply? She would probably say how humbled to be listed in the lineage of the Messiah, Jesus Christ, and how overwhelmed and grateful she was to God. She might even say how amazed she is that now thousands of years later her story is still being told and read by many.

There have been significate decisions in my own life which, at the time, didn't seem of any great importance. My decision to follow and marry my husband, David, was one of the best choices I ever made. The magnitude of that decision has given me an overwhelming joy and gratitude to God for all the wonderful works he continues to do in my life. What a decision!

What decision(s) will we make that may have the power to change the course and destiny of lives forever? Decisions that will impact future generations long after we are dead and gone. Abraham and Ruth never saw the results of their choices, and likewise, we may never see the outcome of our choices either. But, just as their faith in God directed their paths, even so, our faith in God can influence future generations. For it is written, "The steps of a good man are ordered by the Lord." (Psalm 37:23.)

Therefore, let us walk into our tomorrows with faith in God to direct our decisions for the better.

For Your Own Personal Thoughts

Did Not Our Hearts Burn Within Us?

Did Not Our Hearts Burn Within Us?

After Jesus' crucifixion and resurrection, he accompanied two disciples on their way to Emmaus. They conversed the entire walk, not knowing Him. Discouraged that their hopes and dreams seemed gone, Jesus gave them an overview of scripture beginning with Moses and ending with the events they had just experienced. As they neared Emmaus, Jesus left the impression that He would continue his journey; but, they invited, even urged him, to come in, "for it is toward evening, and the day is far spent" (Luke 24:29). As Jesus sat at the table, he blessed and broke the bread and gave it to them. At that instant they recognized him, "And their eyes were opened, and they knew him; and he vanished out of their sight. And they said one to another, Did not our heart burn within us, while he talked with us by the way, and while he opened to us the Scriptures?"(Luke 24:31-32.)

When their eyes were opened to the revelation that he was the Christ, they couldn't get back fast enough to tell the others.

Today does not our heart "burn within us" when He opens our understanding as we commune with Him and read His Word? To realize how much God loves us and wants an intimate relationship with us is such a wonderful revelation.

In the Garden
By C. Austin Miles
Chorus:
And He walks with me, and He talks with me,
And He tells me I am His own;
And the joy we share as we tarry there,
None other has ever known.

Jesus is always present even when we are in dire circumstances. God grieves with us, weeps with us, rejoices with us for He is our hope, and His grace is sufficient in all things.

For Your Own Personal Thoughts

Eternal Weight
of Glory

Eternal Weight of Glory

"For our light afflictions, which is but for a moment, worketh for us a far more exceeding and eternal weight of glory;" (II Corinthians 4:17.)

In my book *50 Year Old Love Letters (A Two-fold Love Story)*, I equated this verse to my courtship of many years ago. The "light afflictions" represented the letters my husband and I had to write to stay in touch while dating, for circumstances were always separating us. And, "which is but for a moment," represented the 2 ½ years we had to write those letters compared to our almost 50 years of marriage. And the "far more exceeding and eternal weight of glory" was when I found the letters after he was gone, and the comfort and hope they brought to my grieving heart.

What are your "light afflictions"? Today it might be the trials you face to overcome health issues, financial limitations, loss of a loved one, or any number of life's problems.

Then the scripture says, "which is but for a moment." But, moments can feel like years when you are waiting on a doctor's diagnosis, anxious about a job situation, working through the grief process of losing a loved one, or just trying to make it through another day.

The last statement reminds us that the "eternal weight of glory" far out exceeds any of man's imaginations. For anything man can dream up, cannot compare with the ultimate glory and grandeur God has prepared in eternity. For the Bible says, "Eye hath not seen, nor ear heard, neither have entered into the heart of man, the things which God hath prepared for them that love him."(I Corinthians 2:9.)

For we must remember that "...for the things which are seen are temporal ("light afflictions"), but the things which are not seen are eternal ("weight of glory"). (II Corinthians 4:18.)

For Your Own Personal Thoughts

Fasting! A Personal Testimony!

Fasting! A Personal Testimony!

I had never fasted in my life until I was seeking what the Bible had to say about baptism in Jesus Name, One God, and in-filling of Holy Ghost. Just a young bride, having been married only a few months, I was pondering the question about being baptized in Jesus Name.

You see, as a young girl I had been baptized in the titles, Father, Son, and Holy Ghost and had experienced repentance, but God's word commands us to be baptized in His Name (Jesus) and experience the gift of the Holy Ghost with the evidence of speaking in tongues. (Acts 2:38).

So my husband suggested I fast and let God show me what I should do. As I fasted, I began to read the Bible (God's way of speaking to us), and God began opening my understanding. The more I read, the more excited I became. When my husband came home from work, I started reading scriptures to him and saying, "Look what it says here in Colossians 1:15, 'Who is the image of the invisible God...' and Colossians 2:9, 'For in him dwelleth all the fullness of the Godhead bodily.' And in I Timothy 3:6, 'God was manifest in the flesh.' And also in Acts 10:44-48, '...And he commanded them to be baptized in the name of the Lord.'"

Through fasting and reading God's word, the scriptures became alive with meaning and understanding. And since that experience of over fifty years ago, I have fasted many times.

If you are seeking God's direction, consider fasting and letting God speak to you through His word, for "they that seek shall find and those who knock it shall be opened unto them."

(See Matthew 7:7.)

For Your Own Personal Thoughts

Finding Wisdom And Understanding (Job 28: 12-28)

Finding Wisdom
And
Understanding
(Job 28: 12-28)

"But where shall wisdom be found?

Man knoweth not the price thereof; neither is it found in the land of the living.

No mention shall be made of coral, or of pearls: for the price of wisdom is above rubies.

The topaz of Ethiopia shall not equal it; neither shall it be valued with pure gold.

Whence then cometh wisdom?"

"And unto man he said, Behold, the fear of the Lord, this is wisdom;"

The word 'fear' means to be in awe or complete reverence of God. If man reverences God, this is wisdom.

"And where is the place of understanding?

Seeing it is hid from the eyes of all living, and kept close from the fowls of the air."

"And unto man he said … and to depart from evil is understanding."

To have understanding is not to associate or be involved with ungodly ways or actions.

God's wisdom is not just 'common sense,' but that man understands and has knowledge of how God works in life and in the earth.

"He that getteth wisdom loveth his own soul: he that keepeth understanding shall find good." (Proverbs 19:8.)

For Your Own Personal Thoughts

Gift of
Repentance

Gift of Repentance

When I read this scripture from Acts 11:18, "…. Then hath God also to the Gentiles granted repentance unto life," I was overwhelmed with gratitude to God for giving us (Gentiles) the gift of repentance also.

How sad our life would be if God had not allowed us repentance, truly a **gift** from Him.

After Jesus' resurrection he came to his disciples, "And said unto them, Thus it is written, and thus it behooved Christ to suffer, and to rise from the dead the third day: and that repentance and remission of sins should be preached in his name among all nations, beginning at Jerusalem." (Luke 24:46-47.) All nations included the Gentiles.

God sent Peter to Cornelius' house to bring the gospel to the Gentiles. "And they of the circumcision which believed were astonished, as many as came with Peter, because that on the Gentiles also was poured out the gift of the Holy Ghost." (Acts 10:45.)

After Peter explained how and why he had gone to the house of Cornelius, the Jerusalem elders acknowledged that God had also extended his **gift** of repentance to the Gentiles. "When they heard these things, they held their peace, and glorified God, saying, Then hath God also to the Gentiles granted repentance unto life." (Acts 11:18.)

Paul and Barnabas returned to Antioch and reported what God had done among the Gentiles. "And when they were come, and had gathered the church together, they rehearsed all that God had done with them, and how he had opened the door of faith unto the Gentiles." (Acts14:27.)

And King David wrote, "Blessed is he whose transgression is forgiven, whose sin is covered. Blessed is the man unto whom the Lord imputeth not iniquity, and in whose spirit there is no guile." (Psalm 32:1-2.)

Repentance. What a marvelous **gift** God has given to us.

For Your Own Personal Thoughts

How Do You Want to be Remembered?

How Do You Want to be Remembered?

As I read through the Old Testament, I began to notice how it recorded the lives of two different men; one identified as "a man after God's own heart," and the other was labeled "the son of Nebat, who made Israel to sin."

"…he raised up unto them David to be their king; and said, I have found David, the son of Jesse, a man after mine own heart" (Acts 13:22).

God called David from tending sheep and made him king of Israel.

Later we read King David made some very bad choices. However, when the prophet exposed his adultery and murder, David said, "I have sinned against the Lord." And the prophet said unto David, "The Lord also hath put away thy sin; thou shalt not die." (II Samuel 12:13.) Psalm 51 is David's prayer of repentance.

God honors a repentant heart. We all have made bad choices now and then, but God forgives a repentant heart.

In contrast, we read about a man named Jeroboam, who became king but caused Israel to sin. We never read where Jeroboam ever repented or turned away from his sins, but only provoked God to anger.

"…and they made Jeroboam the son of Nebat king:" (II Kings 17:21). "Because of the sins of Jeroboam which he sinned, and which he made Israel sin … wherewith he provoked the Lord God of Israel to anger." (I Kings 15:30.) Every time we read about Jeroboam, it always refers to him as "the son of Nebat, who made Israel to sin."

According to these two examples, God remembers us either by a repentant and contrite heart or by an unrepentant heart, rather than by our bad choices.

For God would have forgiven Jeroboam the same as he forgave David, if he had humbled himself and repented for, "The Lord is not slack concerning his promise, as some men count slackness; but is long-suffering to us-ward, not willing that any should perish, but that all should come to repentance." (II Peter 3:9.)

So, we ask ourselves, "How do I want God to remember me?"

For Your Own Personal Thoughts

Jesus is the Constant in My Variable Life

Jesus is the Constant in
My Variable Life

"Jesus Christ the same yesterday, and today, and forever." (Hebrews 13:8)

While earning a degree in Economics, I learned that you can graph all variables except one: **human behavior** for it is unpredictable. In the context of statistics, a variable can have a magnitude of different values under different conditions. With that in mind, we understand human behavior is not predetermined, for life itself is unpredictable daily.

This concept got me to thinking about Jesus and how much he is the anchor in all our life's events and circumstances. For Jesus never changes; He is the center of our world. He is our foundation. Our Rock. Our Strong Tower. Our Peace. Our Joy. Our Everything. He is an ever-present help in time of trouble. (See Psalm 46:1.) Underneath are His everlasting arms. (See Deuteronomy 33:27.)

Why is it so important that Jesus be that constant component in our life? For without Him, all the changes/variables would swell out of control and overwhelm us. With only our human nature to guide us, we would depend on our own understanding and be drawn away by our lusts and desires. Therefore, left on our own, scripture says, "Then when lust hath conceived, it bringeth forth sin: and sin, when it is finished, bringeth forth death." (James 1:15.) And scripture also says that our enemy goes about as a roaring lion, seeking whom he may devour. (See I Peter 5:8.) Left on our own, the enemy can come in like a flood seeking to destroy us through vain imaginations, anxieties, depressions, or condemnation. But scripture says, "Trust in the LORD with all thine heart; and lean not unto thine own understanding. In all thy ways acknowledge him, and he shall direct thy paths." (Proverbs 3:5-6.) What a relief to know that we do not have to rely on our unpredictable human behavior.

When we encounter changes like health and illness, job loss/change, financial crises, heartaches, and hurts, we wonder how we are going to be able to handle it all. Just living every day is unpredictable. Therefore, having Jesus be the constant gives us stability and direction. For he said, "...and lo, I am with you always, even unto the end of the world." (Matthew 28:20.) And Jesus also said, "Come unto me, all ye that labor and are heavy laden, and I will give you rest. Take my yoke upon you.... and ye shall find rest unto your souls. For my yoke is easy, and my burden is light." (Matthew 11:28-30.)

So, "Every good and every perfect gift is from above, and cometh down from the Father of lights, with whom is no variableness, neither shadow of turning." (James 1:17.) What a wonderful feeling to know in all our variable life, Jesus will always be our constant.

For Your Own Personal Thoughts

In the Valley He Restores Our Soul

In the Valley He Restores Our Soul

On the mountaintop, there is victory and what a glorious interval that is in our life. During that time, we are close to heaven, but in the valley, He walks by our side and sometimes even carries us.

I knew a family who had a mountaintop experience in their life by being instrumental in starting a work in a city, and their whole life revolved around the church, and all that was happening in it. For many years this family was the foundation and stability of the church.

Some years later, they were asked to leave the church because of some misunderstandings. Being asked to leave was like a crushing blow to all they held dear. So began their valley that looked like it had no end. And for five years it seemed like it would always be that way. The parents were each going to a different church, and none of their children were going to church at all.

Sometimes when life seems to have taken a turn for the worse, God has ways of making things right again.

Circumstances began to change for the whole family. One moved away and found himself in a new environment and a good church. Also, God did some wonderful things in the lives of the parents as things began to change gradually. The husband and wife were reconciled back into the church by a new pastor. God sent other people who were instrumental in bringing the children back to God also. At the end of their valley experience, God restored, renewed, and refreshed their souls the rest of their lives. Thoughts and feelings started to heal, and a refreshing spirit of God was coming to each of them. Where would we be if it was not for the Lord in our lives?

God is the lifter up of our head, and as the psalmist, David, says, "He restores my soul." (Psalm 23:3.)

Jesus quoted from the Old Testament, "…he hath sent me to heal the brokenhearted …. to set at liberty them that are bruised." (Luke 4:18.)

"But thou, O Lord, art a shield for me; my glory, and the lifter up of my head." (Psalm 3:3.)

Life has a way of bruising our spirits, but God's word gives us the promise that if we will come to Him, He will heal and comfort us. He will refresh our souls and give us a renewed purpose.

For Your Own Personal Thoughts

Leaving this World

Leaving this World

I ask myself the question, where will I be when I leave this world? We have no idea the physical place we will be, but in a spiritual sense, we can know where we stand with God when that time comes.

I thought about the physical place my husband was and also my brother-in-law when they left this world.

Goat Creek Cut-off Road, Kerrville, Texas! This is where my sister's husband left this world. Every day of the week she passes this place on her way to and from work. How many times has she glanced at the pole he hit and has a flashback to that day? Does she shed tears on occasion? What thoughts come to her at different intervals? Does she pass by with other things on her mind and not even think about the spot's significance?

Odessa, Texas at 13310 West County Road 123, David left this world lying in his lift chair. Every day I walk by that place in the sitting room of the house David built for me. Many days I don't even think about that being the spot where, in his sleep, he slipped away into eternity. At times I do think about it and love to stand there in my memories. It is a comfort to think that he was right here at home when he left this world.

Recently there have been family and friends who have lost a loved one. We know where they physically were when they left this world.

But, may we all reflect on our own spiritual position; to know where spiritually we are when God calls us to leave this world.

"Wherefore the rather, brethren, give diligence to make your calling and election sure: …"

(I Peter 1:10a.)

Zion's Hill
By James A Crutchfield
Chorus:
"Someday beyond the reach of mortal ken,
Someday, God only knows just where and when,
The wheels of mortal life shall all stand still,
And I shall go to dwell on Zion's hill."

For Your Own Personal Thoughts

Living for Tomorrow

Living for Tomorrow

"Unto them that look for Him shall he appear the second time without sin unto salvation." Hebrews 9:28

Until Then
by Stuart Hamblin
"My heart can sing when I pause to remember,
A heartache here is but a stepping stone;
Along the trail that's winding always upwards,
This troubled world is not my final home.
The things of earth will dim and lose their value,
If we recall they're borrowed for a while;
And things of earth that cause the heart to tremble,
Remembered there will only bring a smile.

Chorus:
But until then my heart will go on singing,
Until then with joy, I'll carry on,
Until the day my eyes behold the city,
Until the day God calls me home."

God is already in our tomorrow; we will always need Him to go before us. He has promised that he would be with us even unto the end of the world.

"But as it is written, Eye hath not seen, nor ear heard, neither have entered into the heart of man, the things which God hath prepared for them that love him." (I Corinthians 2:9.)

When He returns, will He find us living for tomorrow?

For Your Own Personal Thoughts

Living in the Afterglow

Living in the Afterglow

What is the 'afterglow?'

In Webster's dictionary, afterglow is compared to the splendor and radiance and profusion of soft light after the sun has set.

Perhaps it could be compared to the time after an awesome service, where God's presence was felt in a sweet, quiet and reverent way, and you left with a warm radiant feeling in your heart and soul.

What do you think Peter, James, and John felt as they gazed into the heavens at Christ's transfiguration?

"And after six days Jesus taketh with him, Peter and James, and John … and he was transfigured before them. And his raiment became shining, exceeding white as snow; so as no fuller on earth can white them. …And Peter answered and said to Jesus, Master, it is good for us to be here: … And as they came down from the mountain, he charged them that they should tell no man what things they had seen, till the Son of man were risen from the dead." (Mark 9:2-9.)

Don't you imagine the disciples felt a radiant afterglow as they descended the mountain?

The Bible gives an account of Moses after God had showed him his back parts. Moses had an afterglow on his face from being in the presence of God.

"And he said, I beseech thee, show me thy glory. …" (Exodus 33:18, 22.)

"…when he came down from the mount, that Moses wist not that the skin of his face shone while he talked with him. …And the children of Israel saw the face of Moses, that the skin of Moses' face shone:" (Exodus 34:29.)

The radiance and splendor of an afterglow is only a short duration of time; but, to have experienced a moment like that lives on in our memories.

For Your Own Personal Thoughts

Peace in the Fire

Peace in the Fire

In the center of the ceiling of our church sanctuary is a stain glass octagon with sections marked off with wood beams. Stain glass forms a "flame" of fire in a circle. Intertwining that circle is one with a dove in flight with a twig of an olive branch.

Over the years, as I sat in church, I would gaze up at the big stain glass circle and think it should have a name. So, I started calling it "Peace in the Fire."

The doves represent God's Spirit. There is peace from God that abides within the soul. The flames, the tongues of the Holy Ghost as He fills us with His presence. The flames could also represent trials in our life. However, there is peace in God's presence.

God gives us His peace in our fiery trials. It is that peace that passes all understanding that only He can give. (Philippines 4:7.)

Jesus said, "These things I have spoken unto you, that in me ye might have peace. In the world ye shall have tribulation: but be of good cheer; I have overcome the world." (John 16:33.)

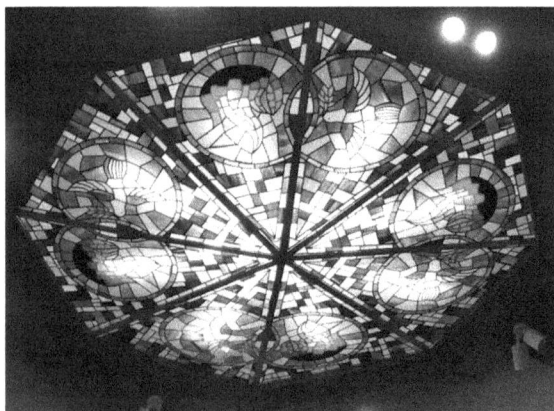

The stain glass octagon in the ceiling of the sanctuary

For Your Own Personal Thoughts

Presumptuous Sins?

Presumptuous Sins?

In Psalm 19, David asks the Lord to keep him from "presumptuous" sins that they would not have dominion in his life.

"Who can understand his errors? Cleanse thou me from secret faults. Keep back thy servant also from presumptuous sins; let them not have dominion over me: ..." (Psalm 19:12.)

What are "presumptuous" sins? I wondered.

Definition from Webster's dictionary says Presumptuous is overweening (excessive self-importance; arrogant) proud or self-confident; taking undue liberties; overbold.

In Matthew 20:2-16, Jesus tells a parable of a householder, which went out early in the morning to hire laborers into his vineyard. And when he had agreed with the laborers for a penny a day, he sent them into his vineyard. At different times during the day, he hired more laborers to work in his vineyard, even up to the last hour of the day. And at the end of the day, he told his steward to call the laborers and pay them, starting with the last even to the first. So the steward gave every man a penny from the last to the first. But they that were hired first supposed they would have received more. And they began to complain, "saying, These last have wrought but one hour, and thou hast made them equal unto us, who have worked all day." But the householder reproved them and reminded them that they had agreed to work for the amount they received. Why should the first think themselves better than the last laborers hired?

In Luke 18:10-14, we read another parable about the Pharisee and the Publican who went to the temple to pray. The Pharisee prayed, "God, I thank thee, that I am not as other men are, extortioners, unjust, adulterers, or even as this publican." Then he reminded the Lord of all the good things he did. But the publican would not even lift his head, "but smote upon his breast, saying, God be merciful to me a sinner." Jesus said that the publican went home justified rather than the other. "for every one that exalteth himself shall be abased; and he that humbleth himself shall be exalted."

I think we can say that both the first hired laborers and the Pharisee were presumptuous. Both were arrogant and overbold.

Paul stated in Romans 12:3 "… to every man that is among you, not to think of himself more highly than he ought to think; but to think soberly, according as God hath dealt to every man the measure of faith."

May we examine ourselves and our attitude toward others? Can we say with King David, "keep back thy servant also from presumptuous sins; let them not have dominion over me."

For Your Own Personal Thoughts

Salvaged Not Totaled

Salvaged Not Totaled

"In whom we have redemption through his blood, the forgiveness of sins, according to the riches of his grace;" (Ephesians 1:7).

It all started with a severe hailstorm that damaged my vehicle and the insurance claim I received. At first, I was upset that my car was classified as "salvaged." But the reality was it was better than being classified "totaled." If the insurance had totaled it, I would have lost the car for it would have been towed to the dump yard; I would have been without a vehicle; would have had to pay off balance owed; and then find another car and start over with payments, probably for another six years.

Being salvaged meant I would get to keep the car. Salvaged, I was able to pay the car off two years early with insurance money that was left after I did not have to have them finish all the final repairs the claim covered. My car looked good in my eyes, but it did hurt a little to think of the stigma man's system had labeled the car. Even though my car still had some damage, I rescued it from being totaled.

The more I thought about all that happened with my car situation, the more I realized in a spiritual sense what God did to redeem us. When sin entered the world, it labeled humanity as "totaled." On the outside, we still looked good, but on the inside, when God looked at the heart, he saw the damage sin had done.

We were classified as "totaled," but in His eyes, we were salvageable for Jesus provided redemption through His death, burial, and resurrection. To obey the gospel, and have the blood of Jesus Christ applied to our lives, we can be classified as "salvaged."

Damaged in transit (totaled) but still deliverable (salvaged). Although sin damaged the human race, God rescued us and made us deliverable from sin through His blood.

"Because of the sacrifice of the Messiah, his blood poured out on the altar of the Cross, we're a free people - free of penalties and punishments chalked up by all our misdeeds. And not just barely free, either. Abundantly free!" (Ephesians 1:7, The Message)

For Your Own Personal Thoughts

Seven Beatitudes (Blessings) of Revelation

Seven Beatitudes (Blessings) of Revelation

Blessing 1:

> Revelation 1:3, "Blessed is he that readeth, and they that hear the words of this prophecy, and keep those things which are written therein: for the time is at hand."

Blessing 2:

> Revelation 14:13, "And I heard a voice from heaven saying unto me, Write, Blessed are the dead which die in the Lord from henceforth: Yea, saith the Spirit, that they may rest from their labors; and their works do follow them."

Blessing 3:

> Revelation 16:15, "Behold, I come as a thief. Blessed is he that watcheth, and keepeth his garments, lest he walk naked, and they see his shame."

Blessing 4:

> Revelation 19:9, "And he saith unto me, Write, Blessed are they which are called unto the marriage supper of the Lamb. And he saith unto me, These are the true sayings of God."

Blessing 5:

> Revelation 20:6, "Blessed and holy is he that hath part in the first resurrection: on such the second death hath no power, but they shall be priests of God and of Christ, and shall reign with him a thousand years."

Blessing 6:

Revelation 22:7, "Behold I come quickly: blessed is he that keepeth the sayings of the prophecy of this book."

Blessing 7:

Revelation 22:14, "Blessed are they that do his commandments, that they may have right to the tree of life, and may enter in through the gates into the city."

What blessings and hope the Lord gives to us if we will only believe and obey.

Read, hear, and keep. Die in the Lord will rest from labors, and their works will follow them.

Watch and keep his garments, so will not be naked or shamed.

God calls unto the marriage supper of the Lamb.

To have part in the first resurrection, will not experience the second death and will be priests of God and Christ reigning a thousand years.

Keep the sayings of the prophecy of this book and do his commandments.

Near the Cross
By Fanny Crosby/W. H. Doane

Near the cross I'll watch and wait,
Hoping, trusting, ever,
Till I reach the golden strand,
Just beyond the river.
Chorus
In the cross, in the cross,
Be my glory ever;
Till my raptured soul shall find
Rest beyond the river.

For Your Own Personal Thoughts

Some Battered Stakes

Some Battered Stakes

"In the world ye shall have tribulation: but be of good cheer; I have overcome the world." John16:33

After reading Brother J.T. Pugh's book, *"The Battered Stake,"* I pondered over his words as he described a "battered stake"; individuals bruised and battered for the gospel's sake. Two families immediately came to mind. Both laid the foundation for the oneness gospel in their perspective cities. The first was in my hometown, and the other in the place I would later call home for fifty years. Those pioneers have long passed away, but what they left behind is a testimony to the glory of God.

One of those families became my in-laws. They moved from Lou Ann, Arkansas, to the booming oilfields in the Texas panhandle. Pampa, Texas became the home of the Butcher family for the rest of their lives. Henry and Fannie Butcher not only brought with them their two small children but also their faith. Standing firm and "contending for the faith" was not always easy and at those times they stood as "battered stakes." Over time, they had many come to preach, but for one reason or the other, they did not stay. Finally, they asked Brother W. H. Massengale to come and pastor. The first service they held in the Butcher's living room at 1245 S. Wilcox. Brother Massengale said, "Well if we're going to have a church I guess we need to pass the offering plate." And they did! From this humble beginning, the church grew in number. As the congregation increased, over time, they purchased a building and moved it to property on Brown Street. The building was located just east of Hobert Street light on the north side of Brown Street. When Brother Frenchman came, they moved the church building to Naida Street, where it stands today.

In Odessa, Texas, like the Butcher's in Pampa, the Callis' became "battered stakes" for the kingdom of God. Brother J. F. Solomon came and held a tent revival in the city. The Callis' received the Holy Ghost during the revival and were baptized in Jesus Name. Through this family, the oneness work continued in Odessa. Land at the corner of Sam Houston and Olive Street was donated, and monies were collected to build a church. The Callis' were instrumental in seeing the building project to completion. This south side congregation grew and later relocated to the corner of Jackson and 19th Street. Many years later, under the pastorate of J. T. Pugh, they built a new building on the corner of Texas and 17th Street, where the church stands today.

Both families endured hardships and persecution through the years as both churches began to win converts. Even after both churches were well established, these families suffered many things in their personal lives. However, both the Butcher's and Callis' endured to the end for "they fought a good fight and they kept the faith."

Today I am personally blessed because of these "battered stakes." First, by marrying into the Butcher family, I found a closer relationship with God. Second, having ended up in Odessa, I have an established church to attend.

In honor of these two families, and others like them, always remember our lives are blessed because of some "battered stakes"?

For Your Own Personal Thoughts

Sweet Smelling Savor

Sweet Smelling Savor

Over and over throughout the book of Leviticus, there is this phrase "sweet-smelling savor unto the Lord." God gave Moses instructions about the sacrifices and offerings Aaron, and his sons were to offer for the children of Israel, and that they were for a "sweet-smelling savor unto the Lord." (See Leviticus 1:9,13, 17; 2:2,9; 3:5,16 ; 4:31 ; 6:15,21 ; 8:21,28 ; 17:6 ; 23:13,18 ; 26:31.)

This phrase caught my attention, and I began to look at other scripture references of a "sweet savor."

The first mention of a "sweet savor" was after the flood when Noah built an altar unto the Lord and offered burnt offerings unto Him. (See Genesis 8:21.)

According to Webster's Dictionary, the word "savor" means "to delight in." The Lord delights in our praises, for it is a "sweet-smelling savor" to him.

Sacrifices under the "Old Covenant" required the shedding of blood and were for cleansing, purifying, and sanctifying.

Following are the sacrifices:

Burnt offering represented submission to God's will.

Sin offering was for propitiation, meaning appeasement for divine justice and reconciliation of man back to God.

Meat/meal offering was to express gratitude and love to God.

Incense offering became the sweet smell of acceptable prayers and intercession to God.

Jesus Christ fulfilled all of these offerings by shedding his blood on the cross as the sacrificial lamb. Therefore he is our mediator to God, so our life can be a "sweet-smelling savor" unto him.

Paul wrote that Christ gave himself for us as an offering and sacrifice to God for a sweet-smelling savor. "And walk in love, as Christ also hath loved us, and hath given himself for us an offering and a sacrifice to God for a sweet-smelling savor." (Ephesians 5:2.)

What a beautiful thought that our life can be a "sweet-smelling savor" unto God.

For Your Own Personal Thoughts

The Big Picture

The Big Picture

When God hangs our "Big Picture" on His enormous wall of eternity and shows us our story from His perspective, we become amazed at his wonderful works to us. He has a way of framing into a picture, our life story after we have experienced some life-changing event. It happened to me when I lost my husband.

Death of a loved one affects our perspective of life and eternity. Shortly after my husband passed away, I found the love letters of our courtship. As I read them, it was as if God rolled a movie screen in front of my face and showed me how God had orchestrated our lives. Putting in place every step for us to meet and even the obstacles that arose, God was still in control of the situation. Before we needed favorable conditions, and special people, God already had them in place. As God unfolded to me how he had worked his plan in my life, gratitude to Him overcame me.

After our loss, we may feel empty at first, but with God, we can have purpose to live. Oh, the big picture of our life is overwhelming when we look back! The scripture in Psalm 107: 8, "Oh, that men would praise the Lord for his goodness; and for His wonderful works to the children of men." I began to think of the "wonderful works" God had done in my life (one of the children of men). God showed me a beautiful story, how so unaware I was, at the time, of anyone else's perspective except my own. Now, I realized what David's folks must have thought, what David must of thought and felt, what my mother must have been going through, and, above all, what God was doing in my life!

When we choose to acknowledge God in all our ways, He directs our path. He writes our story that we could never accomplish alone. "In all thy ways acknowledge him, and he shall direct thy paths." (Proverbs 3:6.) If we look at our circumstances (good or bad) from God's perspective, then we will always see the beauty in life. In our mourning is the beauty of God's comforting Spirit. When we look back, we see a trail of His fingerprints in our circumstances, daily life, choices we have made, and the direction He has taken us. Life to us seems long, but to God our life is less than a blink of the eye. "For what is your life? It is but a vapor, which appears for a little time, and then vanishes away."(James 4:14.)

When I come to the end of my time, I hope my "big picture" will still reflect a beautiful story of abundant life in God. For Jesus said, "…I am come that they might have life, and that they might have it more abundantly." (John 10:10.)

What will your' "Big Picture" look like on God's wall of eternity?

"Being confident of this very thing, that he which hath begun a good work in you will perform it until the day of Jesus Christ:" (Philippines 1:6.)

For Your Own Personal Thoughts

The Unseen Blessings

The Unseen Blessings

An unseen blessing only becomes visible to us when we look back. Sometimes we look at circumstances in our lives and think it's a bad situation, but in reality, it turns out to be a wonderful blessing.

A friend and I talked about a hailstorm of a few years ago that turned out to be an unseen blessing for both of us. She had made a bad choice in vehicles and was having some situations with it that could have been life-threatening. But, because of the hail damage to the vehicle, she was able to get rid of the car and acquire a safer one.

That same hailstorm proved to be an unseen blessing to me, for I was able to pay off my car two years early. We never know what God will use and turn into a blessing for us. His definition of good toward us does not always appear to be a positive event in our life at the time. "And we know that all things work together for good to them that love God, to them who are the called according to his purpose." (Romans 28:8.)

I purchased a $25 gift card that already had $50 loaded on it that neither the cashier nor I was aware of at the time. So several months later when I used the card and the receipt showed there was still money left on it, I didn't think much of it at the time. When I used the card again, and it covered a larger purchase, which was way over $25, I was puzzled. Later I went back to the store and asked to speak to a manager. She looked up information and found that the gift card already had $50 on it when the cashier added my $25 on to it. "Just use it," she said. What an unseen blessing the card turned out to be.

Delays happen to us for different reasons. We forget to set our alarm.

The traffic is heavy, and we find our self in a traffic jam. An emergency at home or office keeps us from leaving on time. But, later, we are told of some accident or other tragic happening that if we had been on time, it would have involved us. The circumstances that happen in our lives God uses as unseen blessings. Only when we are on the other side of the situation, do we realize the blessing in it. "For I know the thoughts I think toward you, saith the Lord, thoughts of peace, and not of evil, to give you an expected end." (Jeremiah 29:11.)

Unseen blessings abound in what seems like our darkest hours. God turns our mourning into dancing and our sorrow into joy. (See Psalm 30:11 and Isaiah 61:3.) Even the disciples did not realize the unseen blessing in Jesus' crucifixion until the day of Pentecost when they received the Holy Ghost as well as 3,000 more after Peter preached. (See Acts 2:41.)

The Disciples biggest disappointment was mankind's greatest victory. They went from grievous disappointment to great rejoicing.

For Your Own Personal Thoughts

Those with the Least, Give the Most

Those with the Least, Give the Most

Those with the least during Bible times were usually widows. Luke records a story of Jesus watching as the people put their offering in the treasury; he observed the widow who dropped in two mites. He turned to his disciples and told them that she had given the most. The others had given out of their abundance, but she had given her all. (Luke 21:1-4.)

In today's world, I have witnessed first-hand, several people, who have given much, even though they have little.

My sister does not have much of this world's goods but has shared what she does have. After her husband passed away, Habitat for Humanities, came and fixed several things around her home. Out of the group, who did the work, one person saw she had a room that needed finishing to be usable. After he completed the room, she thought of the Shunammite woman who built a room on her home for the prophet. My sister saw a need and offered her newly finished room to a couple. They lived with her two and half years before they were able to get back on their feet financially and afford a place of their own.

Psalm 37:16 says, "A little that a righteous man hath is better than the riches of many wicked."

In 1972, my husband and I started going, during the summer, to Tupelo Children's Mansion, an orphanage in Mississippi. "Aunt" Myrtle, as she was known on campus, was over the kitchen. One summer, we went with the Mansion to Louisiana camp meeting. "Aunt" Myrtle had taken out a loan from the bank to go, and on the way back from camp the Mansion, staff, and children stopped at Natchez, MS, for a service.

They took up an offering for the Mansion kids, and she dropped all the money she had left into the offering plate. Her heart was always for the kids and not for herself. Her sacrifice was out of the little she possessed. She was someone who had little but gave much.

Jesus encountered a young man who had much but was not willing to share his abundance with others. "The young man saith unto him, All these things have I kept from my youth up: what lack I yet? Jesus said unto him, If thou wilt be perfect, go and sell that thou hast, and give to the poor, and thou shalt have treasure in heaven: and come and follow me. But when the young man heard that saying, he went away sorrowful: for he had great possessions." (Matthew 19:20-22.)

Those with the most, give the least, it seems.

For Your Own Personal Thoughts

Two Rooms

Two Rooms

This **room of Time** we live in is only the vestibule of our life; the largest part we'll live in the **room of Eternity.**

While we occupy the **room of Time,** we fill it with the joys and sorrows of life. "To everything there is a season, and a time to every purpose under the heaven: a time to be born, and a time to die; ….a time to weep, and a time to laugh; a time to mourn, and a time to dance;" (Ecclesiastes 3:1-2, 4). Therefore, we laugh, cry, grieve, rejoice, and enjoy living in this earthly atmosphere. God determines the length of our life in this **room of Time**, but we, by our experiences and choices, give life its meaning and depth. Will we then be able to say, "O death, where is thy sting? O grave, where is thy victory?" (I Corinthians 15:55.)

The **room of Eternity** is so much more glorious than this **room of Time.** "For since the beginning of the world men have not heard, nor perceived by the ear, neither hath the eye seen, O God, beside thee, what he hath prepared for him that waiteth for him." (Isaiah 64:4.) I have tried to imagine that room where loved ones reside, but my human mind cannot grasp the splendor and beauty of that place. Will everything be intensified: emotions deeper and stronger; colors extremely brilliant, to the extent of colors we have never seen before; and will our senses of touch, smell, see, and hear be highly sensitive to all that will surround us? In Revelation, John tried to describe what he saw: streets transparent gold, light brighter and more glorious than the sun, for the Lamb is the light. "And the city had no need of the sun, neither of the moon, to shine in

it: for the glory of God did lighten it, and the Lamb is the light thereof."
(Revelation 21:23.)

The words to this song expresses how we might feel when we step inside the gate of that **room of Eternity** on the other side of life.

Inside the Gate
By J.D. Sumner
"Oh how happy I will be when life's journey here is run;
And I look upon His face, and I hear Him say "Well done,
You have fought a faithful fight,
And my child you've kept the faith,
Enter now; My joys are yours, so just step inside the gate."

Because, "As it is written, eye hath not seen, nor ear heard, neither have entered into the heart of man, the things which God hath prepared for them that love him." (I Corinthians 2:9).

The grave is a closed-door to this **room of Time** and an open gate to **the room of Eternity**.

For Your Own Personal Thoughts

When We Open Our Bible

When We Open Our Bible
"O taste and see that the Lord is good." Psalm 34:8

Even Jeremiah said, "Thy words were found, and I did eat them; and thy word was unto me the joy and rejoicing of mine heart: for I am called by thy name, O Lord God of hosts." (Jeremiah 15:16.)

We could even say God spreads a meal before us when we open His word and glean crumbs/blessings from the Master's table. What comfort and joy we receive at the Lord's bountiful table. We quietly wait for Him to speak to our spirit and then share with others the wonderful thoughts and ideas he drops into our heart through His word. No other book lifts our spirits, feeds our souls, lights our pathway, and guides our footsteps. Daily the Word of God is the only book we need, for it is a never-ending source of wealth and comfort in all life's situations.

From Genesis to Revelation, His word blesses us. Take Genesis, Numbers, and I and II Chronicles, and we find rich and deep wisdom in the discourse of genealogies, which gives us the knowledge that all humanity comes from God. Then even though we view Leviticus as a rather boring book, in reality, it magnifies the redemptive plan of God and reveals what Jesus Christ did when he became the sacrificial lamb for us. In this way, we could take each book of the Bible and glean something that would speak to our grief, loss, and trials. For in His Word, we find mercy and grace.

Someone came up with an acronym of the word "Bible";

B- basic
I- instruction
B- before
L- leaving
E- earth.

Even some of our U.S. Presidents acknowledged the importance of the Bible in our lives. The following quotes are found in the book "The Rebirth of America" on page 37.

"The first and almost the only Book deserving
of universal attention is the Bible."
John Quincy Adams

"All the good from the Saviour of the world is communicated through this Book; but for the Book, we could not know right from wrong. All the things desirable to man are contained in it."
Abraham Lincoln

"...the Bible...is the one supreme source of revelation of the meaning of life, the nature of God and spiritual nature and need of men. It is the only guide of life which really leads the spirit in the way of peace and salvation."
Woodrow Wilson

"Go to the Scriptures...the joyful promises it contains
will be a balsam to all your troubles."
Andrew Jackson

"The foundations of our society and our government rest so much on the teachings of the Bible that it would be difficult to support them if faith in these teachings would cease to be practically universal in our country."
Calvin Coolidge

So let us, as Jeremiah did, eat (read/devour) His words, and they will be joy and rejoicing to our hearts for He calls us by His name. Praise God!

For Your Own Personal Thoughts

Women in the
Bible Who
Saved the Day

Women in the Bible Who
Saved the Day

Have you ever thought about the bravery of some women mentioned in the Bible? Through their actions, they saved the day, not only for themselves but for others as well.

The first that comes to mind is Esther, Hadassah's Persian name. She was a beautiful Jewish maiden orphaned and brought up in the household of her cousin, Mordecai. He held an office in King Ahasuerus' (known as Xerxes in history) court in the Persian Empire. Through the dethronement of Queen Vashti, Esther was chosen to become queen. Mordecai had cautioned her not to let her parentage or race be known. Later, King Ahasuerus, unaware of what he was doing, gave Haman authority to have all Jews killed. Mordecai informed Esther of the decree and said, "You may have come to the kingdom for such a time as this." (Esther 4:14.) Even though the king had not summoned her, she risked her life when she entered the court. For the law was that whosoever came into the court without being summoned, unless the king held out the golden scepter to them, could be killed. Through Esther's courage, her life and the life of her people, the Jews, were spared. Therefore, we can say she saved the day for the Jews and turned what would have been a tragic time into rejoicing. Even today, the Jewish people celebrate what is called Purim yearly, which corresponds to our calendar year, February/March.

Next, we think of Ruth, who lived during the last years of the Judges, possibly during Gideon or Eli's rule. After Naomi, her mother-in-law was left a widow and childless, Ruth followed her back to Bethlehem. They returned to the land of Judah at the beginning of barley harvest. Ruth went to glean in the fields of Boaz, a wealthy near kinsman of Elimelech, her deceased father-in-law. Over time, Boaz performed the part of a near kinsman by purchasing Elimelech's inheritance, which included taking Ruth as his wife. Again we see the courage of a woman who left all that was familiar to her and entered a land unfamiliar to her. But because she was willing to go, Ruth, a Moabite was adopted into the family of Israel and is named in the lineage of the Messiah, Jesus Christ, through her son, Obed, who she bore to Boaz.

How dangerous was the actions of Rahab, the harlot, who protected the Israelite spies that came into the city of Jericho? She not only hid them but also helped them escape. Because of this, she and her family were saved out of the destruction of Jericho. (see Joshua 2.) And scripture says, "By faith the harlot, Rahab perished not with them that believed not, when she had received the spies with peace." (Hebrews 11:31.), and, "Was not Rahab the harlot justified by works, when she had received the messengers and had sent them out another way?" (James 2:25.) Rahab's decision took courage when she chose to hide the spies, hang the scarlet cord out her window on the wall, and remain in her house with her family. She saved the day for she and her family by her actions. Therefore, changing she and her family's destiny.

These women's bravery was astounding, but when we think of what Mary, the mother of Jesus, was willing to do, our hearts are overwhelmed. What if she had not been willing to submit to God's plan to redeem the whole human race? I am sure God would have used someone else, but Mary was willing, not knowing all the heartache that would be associated with her decision. After Jesus' birth, Joseph and Mary took him to the Temple to do for him according to the law. There she was told by Simeon that a sword would pierce her own heart. (Luke 2:34-35.) And Mary pondered in her heart the things told her. Later, she would experience the heart-wrenching pain as she watched the crucifixion of Jesus. In a sense, we could say she helped save the world.

For Your Own Personal Thoughts

Year of Jubilee

Year of Jubilee

Several months after my husband passed away, I was reading in Leviticus about the jubilee year they were to celebrate every 50th year and what the people were to do during that year. I decided that even though David passed away eight months before our 50th Wedding Anniversary, I would celebrate and call it my "Year of Jubilee."

The Jubilee Year? How was it calculated? Why was it to be celebrated?

For six years, Israelites were to plant and harvest their fields and vineyards, and the 7th year would be declared a Sabbath Year in which they did not sow and reap. (See Leviticus 25:3-4.) They were to do this seven times, which brought them to the 49th year, a Sabbath Year. Then followed the 50th year, the Year of Jubilee, another Sabbath Year. (See Leviticus 25:8, 11.) Therefore, when the jubilee came, there were three years before another harvest, but God promised to make the sixth year produce enough to sustain them for those three years. (See Leviticus 25:21.)

But, Israel never completely celebrated the jubilee as the Lord had instructed. Therefore, it was foretold by the prophet that they would go into exile for seventy years: a year in exile for every jubilee year they had not observed. (See II Chronicles 36:21, and Jeremiah 25:11-12.) But, God is merciful and gracious and promised that after the land had enjoyed her Sabbaths, he would allow the exiles to return. (See Jeremiah 29:10.)

Around the first of October was the Feast of Trumpets, which ushered in the Jubilee and the Feast of Tabernacles. This event was to be a special time of joy, celebration, and rest. (See Zechariah 14:16.) So many events in my life had occurred in October: my birthday; my Mother's birthday; month David passed away; during our courtship, we had broken up, and it was in October we made up. Besides, October is one of the most beautiful times of the year. Since Jubilee represents 50 years and would have been 50 years of marriage, I thought it unique to call it "My Year of Jubilee."

I gave a reception to honor and celebrate the wonderful marriage God gave us and had a display of memorabilia from our 50 years together. Even though there was grief in losing my husband, there was also joy in remembering all that I'd had for 50 years. My sister, Cathy, introduced the event by quoting Leviticus 25:9-12, "Then shalt thou cause the trumpet of the jubilee to sound ….throughout all your land. And ye shall hallow the fiftieth year ….A jubilee shall that fiftieth year be unto you: ….it shall be holy unto you:"

And just as God had promised an abundant harvest during a jubilee, he has provided an abundant harvest in my life in the years since David's passing. To me the most outstanding accomplishment is my book, *50 Year-old Love Letters (A Two-fold Love Story)*. I still am amazed at how God orchestrated events for me to have my memoirs recorded and become a published author. He has blessed me with good health, wonderful siblings, sufficient finances, and spiritual blessings innumerable.

My Jubilee Year became a time of restoration and renewal as I worked through my grief, knowing our future Jubilee awaits in eternity.

For Your Own Personal Thoughts

The WOW Factor

The WOW Factor

We have patriotic feelings on July 4th as we watch the night sky light up with splashes of fireworks, the bursts of multicolored canopies as they sparkle like tiny stars. The ooh's and ah's as we watch the colors explode overhead. It WOW's us!

We are also WOWed by holiday feelings that seem to usher in Thanksgiving and Christmas festivities; preparations for that Thanksgiving dinner, and the feelings of "peace and goodwill" come floating on the air as we listen to Christmas carols. Our hearts swell as we think of family and friends we will be with during the holiday season. We say, WOW!

But above and beyond those WOW's in our lives, God has prepared a WOW, "eye has not seen, nor ear heard neither hath entered into the heart of man." (I Corinthians 2:9.)

WOW! WOW! WOW!

Takes our breath away, just thinking of it!

When we begin to read of streets of gold, (Revelation 21:21.)

Walls of jasper, (Revelation 21:18.)

City whose foundation is of precious jewels, (Revelation 21:19.)

And gates of pearl. (Revelation 21:21.)

The Tree of Life bears twelve different kinds of fruit. (Revelation 22:2.)

The River of Life runs through the midst of the city. (Revelation 22:1.)

The New Jerusalem compared as to a bride adorned for her husband. (Revelation 21:2.)

The Lamb is the Light, for there is no night there. (Revelation 21:23.)

Add to all that, the majesty and glory of His throne; the glassy sea; and a complete rainbow. (Revelation 4:3, 6)

Our human mind cannot comprehend or contain all the WOW that awaits us.

The real WOW factor is yet to come.

For Your Own Personal Thoughts

www.ingramcontent.com/pod-product-compliance
Lightning Source LLC
Chambersburg PA
CBHW051825090426
42736CB00011B/1653